FORT WORTH PUBLIC LIBRARY

3 1668 02774 6871

Call Center
Benchmarking

W9-AAI-664

Customer Access Management
Jon Anton, Series Editor

Call Center Benchmarking

How Good Is "Good Enough"

by Jon Anton and David Gustin

assisted by Stijn Spit

Ichor Business Books
An Imprint of
Purdue University Press
West Lafayette, Indiana

FORT WORTH PUBLIC LIBRARY

Copyright © 2000 by Purdue University Press. All rights reserved.

Printed in the United States of America

Library of Congress Cataloging-in-Publication Data
Anton, Jon.
    Call center benchmarking : deciding if good is good enough / by
Jon Anton and David Gustin ; assisted by Stijn Spit.
        p. cm.
    Includes bibliographical references and index.
    ISBN 1-55753-215-X (alk. paper)
    1. Call centers—United States—Management. 2. Benchmarking
(Management)—United States. I. Gustin, David, 1962– . II. Title.

HG1616.C29 A57 2000
658.8'12—dc21   00-027224

Contents

Foreword

As the "lightning rod" for customer interactions, world-class call centers are the single point of contact for customers. According to research conducted at Purdue University and Ameritech, over 75% of customer interactions will occur through the call center and the Internet by the year 2003. Fueled by tremendous advances in the integration of telephone and computer technologies, the call center has the potential for being the company's most potent weapon for maintaining long-term customer relationships. The authors of this book have captured the essence of the methodology of benchmarking and presented it in a form that encourages a high-level of self-assessment.

For many companies, global competition has reduced products to mere commodities that are difficult to differentiate through features, functions, or price. Having reached parity, where price and quality are the "table stakes" of doing business, the paradigm shift is definitely toward customer *accessibility.* Executives are beginning to recognize the potential of the call center as a significant revenue generator, perhaps one of the surest investments they can make in enhancing and creating customer value and bottom-line profits. Return on investments made in customer accessibility is seldom less than 100% in the first year and frequently even more if customer lifetime value is included in the equation.

Herein lies the challenge and the primary reason to benchmark your call center metrics against not only the best-in-the-world, but also your most direct competitors, i.e., best-in-class. This book describes in practical terms the ins and outs of benchmarking. I strongly recommend this book to individuals that are striving to enhance the performance of their call centers.

Ray Banas, Director
Ameritech Call Center Consulting Group

1

Introduction

Today's line managers and corporate executives have an overwhelming amount of information available to them to aid in the decision-making process. Since key competitors might also have access to the same information, no one can afford to ignore data sources that might prove useful in obtaining a competitive edge. Although alert managers are constantly seeking new information, they must also learn how to rapidly interpret, integrate, and internalize new information in order to be best-in-class and competitive (Czarnecki 1999). Benchmarking to determine best practices has become an indispensable skill set for many companies in order to maintain their competitive advantage over other companies in their industries. A useful source of current call center performance information can be found at the Purdue University benchmark research website at <http://www.e-Interactions.com>.

The Business Systems Group of Xerox Corporation pioneered benchmarking in the 1970s. The concept originated from reverse engineering of competitors' products and processes and was a major strategic response of Xerox to the increasing level of international competition in the photocopier market. Fortunately, Xerox was willing to share its successes with benchmarking with other companies. Now companies from all over the world and from every industry are using benchmarking to identify best-in-class business practices, which, when implemented correctly, lead to exceptional performances.

This book will focus on the use and the importance of benchmarking in the United States call center industry and will address the following questions:

1. What is benchmarking?
2. What areas can call centers focus on to conduct a benchmark study?
3. How can call centers use internal benchmark data?
4. How can call centers conduct a benchmark study of their own?

2

Benchmarking Defined

Over the past decades several definitions of benchmarking have come to existence. All are interesting, but we will offer only three below:

1. "Benchmarking is a sophisticated method of pinpointing areas of improvement in every business process" (Schwartz 1998).

2. "Benchmarking is the search for industry best practices that lead to superior performances" (Davis and Davis 1994).

3. For the purpose of this book, we would like to define benchmarking as a structured and analytical process of continuously identifying, comparing, deploying, and reviewing best practices worldwide to gain and maintain competitive advantage.

Best practices refer to business practices that outperform all other business practices in any specific industry. In other words, there are no other organizations that perform those practices better. Best practices can be achieved through innovation inside the organization. However it is likely that most innovations have already been discovered and implemented elsewhere. So in order to achieve best practices in your call center, you might want to look beyond the walls of your own organization to see what others are doing (Anton 1997). Benchmarking is the methodology to assist you in doing so. One should keep in mind, though, that benchmarking with partners who are less than best-in-class may lead to improved performance but will never make you reach the highest level of performance increase possible.

Of all the benchmarking methodologies, the two most widely used are competitive benchmarking and process benchmarking. If you are trying to position your performance rank within your industry, competitive benchmarking is the best bet. With competitive benchmarking you measure the performance of your call center directly against that of your competitors.

Process benchmarking, by contrast, measures business processes or practices that are important to the performance of your call center and does this across industries. This type of benchmarking identifies best practices used, regardless of your position in the industry, and proceeds with a thorough study of the processes and the implementation of these practices in your call center.

Service and manufacturing companies have undertaken a rapid investment in call center technologies in recent years. The reason is simple. Practically all customers have a phone, which can be used to securely identify the caller. This enables a win-win situation. The customer has added convenience (around the clock service, trained operators) and the company can service the customer's transaction for presumably a lower cost than other alternatives.

Most companies now offer some phone services to some or

their entire customer base. For large service organizations, multiple call centers can be embedded in each line of business (LOB). For example, for banks you may have dedicated call centers in mortgages, credit cards, installment loans, trust, etc., to service the unique requirements of that LOB.

Why Benchmarking?

Call centers have undergone tremendous changes over the past several years. Once used primarily for inbound-call customer support and help desk functions, the call center is now becoming a dynamic customer contact center, embracing fax, e-mail, and Web communications, in addition to telephone contact. All these changes require constant evaluation of new technologies, procedures, human resource practices, etc. At a recent call center forum sponsored by Global Business Intelligence, the questions were both diverse and indicated the need for some intelligence gathering:

> *Although the number of Internet-based call centers is not currently impressive, we expect it simply to be a matter of time before the Internet is used routinely. What do we need to prepare for?*
>
> *What are some of the innovative service offerings leading organizations are applying to provide superior service?*
>
> *The things that I would like to know center around the fact that everyone talks about world class . . . but what did these organizations do to get there?*
>
> *What did better performing organizations do without investing huge sums into technology; what smart ways do people go about their business?*

How important is the selection of CSOs, and what new techniques and trends are emerging?

What opportunities exist to widen the margin between meeting service levels and sales targets and the need to run cost-effective channel-balancing CSO costs and telecommunication costs?

Benchmarking is not just copying or catch-up, neither is it spying or industrial espionage, and it definitely is not quick and easy to accomplish. So why would you, or should you, benchmark your call center?

First of all, benchmarking can be effective at all levels of call center operations. The idea behind benchmarking is simple: the most effective way to implement changes is by learning from positive experiences that others have had in the past. Benchmarking helps you to

1. expose areas where improvement is needed,
2. pinpoint areas for cost reduction,
3. assess performance objectively,
4. and test whether your improvement initiatives have been successful.

Furthermore, benchmarking encourages striving for perfection and innovative thinking; it can help you to create a better understanding of your industry, and it is the most effective tool to identify best-in-class business practices with a view to their adoption. If you want to calculate the gap between how your call center is performing and how your call center wants to perform, benchmarking is *the* measurement tool to help you find out, because a better understanding of your industry will lead to innovative thinking, and you will be able to achieve your desired level of performance more rapidly.

Benchmarking does not limit itself by only looking at competitive information. It eliminates the guesswork by studying the existing processes and enablers that will lead to best practices, and it encourages innovation by looking outside your industry's zone of comfort.

The focus in benchmarking is to improve one's business operations by learning from the experience of other companies. Benchmarking is a discipline that will help your company to

- understand if your operations costs are above, below, or at the average for various customer-related processes given your technology and size (i.e., scale);
- identify efficiency and effectiveness reasons for improving cost performance;
- focus lessons learned in how companies successfully or unsuccessfully deploy technology, thereby accelerating improvement by bypassing the learning curve and capitalizing on the experiences of others;
- surface new ideas in your organization that have been proven elsewhere and hence will be easier to sell in your own organization; and
- motivate people to change by providing a measure of the gap between a business's current performance and best-in-class performance.

In addition, outsourcing your call center should always be an option unless considered a core competency by your organization.

Outsourcing customer service may not seem intuitive, but there are many reasons why it is done:

- scale of provider,
- experience of provider, and
- faster implementation of new technologies.

By having access to benchmarked information, you can compare your own organization against the outsourcing options in a much more disciplined manner.

A Word of Caution

There is a tendency amongst all management levels to get tied up in all the statistical details that a benchmarking exercise can bring. Data on abandonment rates, service levels, calls per agent, etc., can be interesting, but data alone will not improve your operation. Take caution in comparing just data for a number of reasons:

1. Don't confuse exchanging performance measures with benchmarking. Statistics cannot be improved, but the operations or processes that those statistics purport to measure can.

2. Data regarding averages can be misleading. Your service levels may be 80% of calls within 60 seconds, but is that measured by half-hour, hour, or some other time increment (say, average throughout the day)? From our experience, it is just as important to measure consistency to standards in addition to the standards themselves. All this means is that we have to watch the data source and understand how the re-

searchers gathered the data and drew their conclusions. It also means that the researchers have to understand the complexity of the call center environment. Without that understanding they may draw the wrong conclusions.

3. Call centers typically devote people and budgets to find and incorporate best practices. The problem is that many times it is hard to tell if what was discovered is "best practice" or simply just a practice.

To illustrate the point with a story, one of our clients decided to reduce toiletry expenses by allocating two rolls of toilet tissue a month to staff and eliminating toilet tissue from all bathrooms. All staff members kept tissue at their desks and had to bring the tissue with them when they went to the bathroom. While this policy certainly did reduce waste and theft costs of toilet paper, it will not go down in employee morale laurels as a great cost-savings practice. To me, this is a great story about the difference between following others who have mastered a procurement best practice and people who are simply feeling their way through by trial and error.

Hallmarks of Success

Depending on how and where it is used, we can easily conclude that benchmarking does work. You don't need rainbows to strike it rich. As the following examples show, benchmarking can deliver substantial financial benefits.

Dana Commercial Credit (DCC) increased its return on equity and assets more than 45% since it began benchmarking in 1992. Initially, DCC focused its efforts mostly on customer satisfaction scores but today focuses on every possible identifiable business process. "As a result of benchmarking, we've got a better focus in terms of what we have to do to be successful," Jim Beckham, DCC's quality director, stated.

Sprint focused its benchmarking efforts on cycle time and managed to reduce costs and increase revenues significantly, and Raytheon managed to get a $4.5 million return on its $580,000 investment.

The above-mentioned examples indicate that benchmarking can be a very powerful tool to increase performance and strengthen competitive advantages. One must first understand, however, what areas to benchmark and how. The following chapters will focus on

1. possible areas to benchmark in your call center,

2. the steps necessary to benchmark your call center against other call centers,

3. and the interpretation of the resulting benchmark data.

3

Areas to Benchmark
in Your Call Center

As stated in the previous chapter, benchmarking can be very effective at every level within your organization. Today's companies have an ever increasing amount of data available to them. It can be very difficult to see the forest for the trees; therefore, this chapter focuses on how to selectively pick areas within your call center that, through benchmarking, can yield the highest results.

Within call centers there are multiple areas of operation that can be very interesting for benchmarking purposes. This chapter will focus on nine frequently used benchmark areas, providing you with their descriptions, and selected metrics to compare when benchmarking. We will also demonstrate some benchmarking results from our 1999 Purdue University Call Center Benchmark Study. This study was co-sponsored by Ameritech and the Ernst & Young Customer Solutions Center.

Purdue has conducted a nationwide call center benchmark study for the last four consecutive years. These studies allow you to compare your call center performance not only to world-class practices but also industry-specific best-in-class metrics. The call center metrics to be discussed in this chapter can be grouped into the following categories:

1. center costs,
2. performance metrics,
3. caller satisfaction,
4. center strategy,
5. human resources,
6. call-flow work processes,
7. caller knowledge and agent knowledge,
8. technology integration, and
9. facilities.

Call Center Costs

Call center costs include all costs (fixed and variable) associated with the operations of a call center. Our experience finds a wide variety in how expenses are reported and the manner in which expenses are allocated. For example, one call center may pay most expenses directly to its cost codes (e.g., agent salaries, benefits, corporate training charge-outs, audits, etc.), while another call center may only pay a portion of those direct expenses, and others are maintained at some other corporate or departmental cost code.

For benchmarking purposes the following metrics are appropriate in comparing your call center to others in your industry. Consider the following cost factors when designing your benchmark study:

1. costs related to human resources, such as agent salary, benefits, recruitment, screening, and training;
2. costs related to your network provider;
3. costs related to your computer hardware and software;
4. costs related to your telecommunications equipment;
5. real estate costs;
6. corporate overhead costs, such as legal, audit, human resources, etc. (note: these costs can be 5 to 30% of a total call center budget);
7. comparisons of annual budgets for your call center; and
8. the average cost for an inbound toll-free call.

Assessing Cost Structure Differences

Call center costs typically break down as follows:

- staff (typically 50 to 65% of operations costs),
- telecommunications (typically 25%), and
- IT and telephone systems.

In any benchmarking cost analysis, it is important to measure major cost drivers to assess the impact they have on differences in costs, service, quality, etc. Costs can differ drastically between companies and are impacted primarily by the following demand and supply factors:

Demand Drivers

- Transactions (or scale)
- Products supported and services offered
- Customer mix
- Service level requirements
- Service differentiation

Supply Drivers

- Choice of location
- Agent configuration (e.g., by product, by process, team size, etc.)
- Use of VRU vs. agents
- Staff skills/training
- Staff productivity and loyalty
- Technology (interfaces, systems, desktop, online knowledge available, etc.)
- Network routing methods for workload balancing
- Culture of continuous improvement of processes

Typically, costs are measured by some form of cost per queue, whether the queue be an inbound service call, an inbound sales call, an inbound problem resolution queue, an inbound account maintenance queue, or some other queue structure (for example, one based on customer value).

Examples Driving Cost per Call Differences

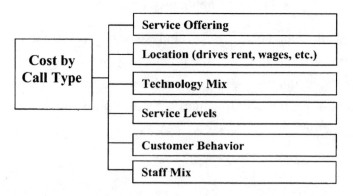

Normalizing Cost Data for Location Differences

In benchmarking, it is important to show the differences between call centers due to productivity and technology efficiency independent of location (because you can be just as inefficient in a low-cost location as a high-cost one). In order to do this, expense data is normalized. Normalizing data is just a way of leveling the playing field for labor and rental costs so one can truly look at efficiency differences. For example, a call center operation in Rochester, N.Y., will have much lower rental and labor costs than one in San Francisco. By adjusting the data, one can then make comparisons based on key drivers of operations.

For example, salary and benefits expenses may be $22,000 per agent in Rochester and $28,000 in San Francisco. Rent per square foot may also be 60% higher in San Francisco. Any cost analysis needs to adjust for the fact that San Francisco's operation has compensation expenses that are 27% higher (and remember, compensation typically is 50% of overall costs) and rents that are 60% higher. The method to do this is to adjust all company data for rent and labor costs to an average and then make cost comparisons, thus eliminating location as a variable for efficiency.

Call Center Performance Measures

When focusing on performance related to the call center efficiency, you can compare the following metrics:

1. average speed of answer,
2. average talk time,
3. average after call work time,
4. average abandonment rate,

5. average time before abandoning,

6. average time in queue,

7. percent of calls blocked,

8. sales per hour, and

9. the number of inbound and outbound calls
   made per agent per shift.

We can go overboard in measuring call center efficiency. In many businesses, abandonment rate can be misleading. The usual assumptions are that there must be industry standards for abandonment and that abandonment is a good indicator of call center performance. But neither is true.

For one thing, abandonment is tough to forecast, at least with any consistent level of accuracy. The conventional wisdom is that longer queues translate into higher abandonment. But caller tolerance to wait is complex and generally is impacted by several factors, including

- degree of motivation for the call;
- availability of substitutes;
- competitors' service level (this can include other financial service companies—banks, insurance, investments, etc.—or other service companies—couriers, airlines, etc.);
- level of expectation;
- time available (this obviously is highly unpredictable); and
- who's paying for the call.

Because of this, service level (defined as calls answered within a specified number of seconds) is the key measure of accessibility.

When focusing on performance related to call center effectiveness, you can compare the following metrics:

1. caller satisfaction,
2. percent of "first-time-final" calls,
3. percent of calls that result in a complaint,
4. percent of calls that result in a sale,
5. average sale value of a call,
6. average sales value generated per agent per year, and
7. the percentage of calls that give rise to up-sell or cross-sell opportunities.

Caller Satisfaction Measurement

Today's world-class call centers are changing from their past fixation on agent productivity to a new fixation on call quality. A very important measure, call quality is the perception the caller had of the call, namely, caller satisfaction. It is much cheaper to retain a customer than to recruit a new one, so call centers are striving for caller loyalty.

Benchmarking within this area provides your call center with information about the current status of customer satisfaction measurements at other companies. Metrics to focus on are the frequency with which call centers measure caller satisfaction, and the ways that satisfaction is measured. The following graph displays world-class averages taken from the Purdue Benchmark Study.

How Do You Measure Caller Satisfaction In-House?

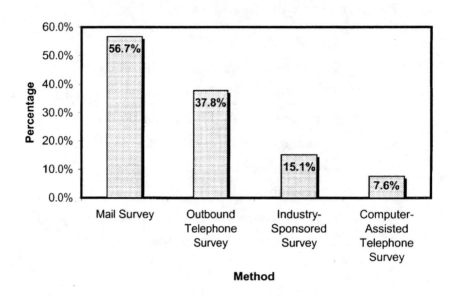

(Source: Purdue University Call Center Benchmark Study, ©1999)

Part of achieving caller satisfaction is understanding how to take a unified customer view across the organization. Organizations are structured based on lines of business, and it is difficult to conduct profitable cross selling or cross servicing unless a unified view of the customer is known. While the technical details behind providing a full corporate view to an operator are quite challenging, one of the key elements of benchmarking is to more fully understand how companies are thinking about this topic and what actions are being taken to create accessible, real-time customer relationship information.

In fact, many smaller institutions that are not encumbered with organization silos for making decisions regarding operating systems, CTI, data warehouses, etc., are providing the lead in this area.

Call Center Strategy

Strategy incorporates every aspect of your call center's vision, its mission, and your goals.

You might want to compare the following:

1. how management views your call center,
2. the percentage of total customer contact handled by your call center instead of being handled by other channels, and
3. types of customer relationship strategies.

One key point is how the call center is treated from a profit or cost perspective. Is the call center treated as

- a business unit with its own P & L?
- a cost center that charges out for services rendered?
- a delivery channel only for specific customers or products?
- a cost center that does not charge out for services rendered?

The manner in which a call center is treated speaks volumes to how the business is managed.

We find that there is a direct correlation to profit/cost treatment and what key information is collected, what information is reported to senior management, and what impact this has on major decisions.

A company's call center strategy can emphasize one or more of the following categories, but not all of them, since tradeoffs must be made.

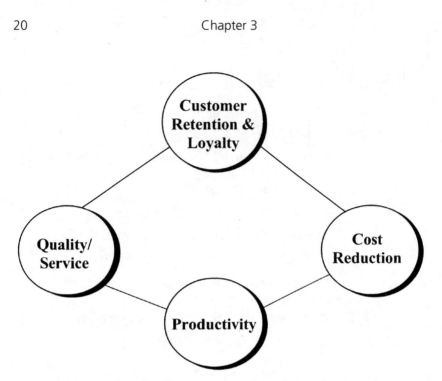

An example of call center benchmark results in this area is shown below.

How Does Management View Your Call Center?

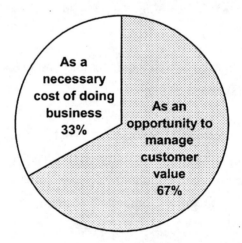

(Source: Purdue University Call Center Benchmark Study, ©1999)

Human Resource Management

The human resource management is responsible for every aspect of the call center where people are involved. People are the call center's most valuable asset and, at the same time, the call center's most costly line item (accounting for over 50% of most call center budgets).

Staff management processes are at the core of a call center. We break staff management processes into six groupings and find there are several areas worth comparing your call center with other companies.

Major Staff Management Processes

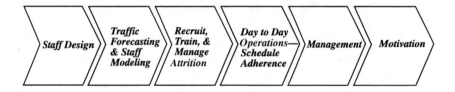

Staff Design

Staff design speaks to how you build a job in the call center, how you configure your staff, and what different types of call agents you have. As you can see on the following page, Purdue's Benchmarking database shows that 35% of agents trained are specialized versus 65% universal.

While industry certainly drives this data, another slice is how many agents are asked to do both inbound and outbound calling. Some organizations ask their inbound agents to do outbound calls (e.g., fund collections, marketing campaigns, etc.) during downtime, while others feel outbound calling effort is so different that it warrants its own specialists.

**What Percentage of Your Agents Is Trained
to Be Specialized Versus Universal?**

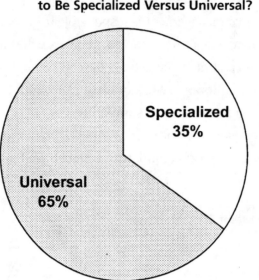

Source: Purdue University Call Center Benchmark Study, ©1999)

Traffic Forecasting and Staff Modeling

Many call centers use some automated workforce software and his-
torical and forecasted data to predict staffing levels, control idle time,
and ensure service level targets are achieved. These models can be
inaccurate at times (poor data, unpredicted turnover, etc.), and sharing benchmarking information on how to improve forecasting is
quite helpful.

Recruit, Train, and Manage Staff Attrition

This is probably the single biggest area under human resource practices where information sharing can bring tremendous results. Many
banks now use behavioral models to recruit and place staff (inbound
service vs. inbound sales, conflict resolution, etc.). Comparing these
models and their relative performance in predicting tenure can be

part of that 1% difference when you are recruiting hundreds of staff members a year.

For example, in Global Business Intelligence's general banking call center study, we found the majority of staff tenure for inbound sales agents to be less than one year at four institutions where detailed data was collected. This is obviously a concern, as asking agents to be familiar with sales desktop technology, product information, and sales and objection techniques is not something that can be learned in six months. Only one bank had the average staff tenure exceeding one year, and, not surprisingly, it also had the most effective new accounts per sales rep ratio.

Staff Tenure — Inbound Sales Agents
Major U.S. Banking Institutions

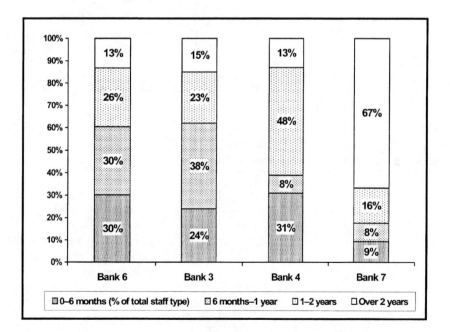

(Source: Global Business Intelligence Benchmark Study, ©1999)

Bank Call Center	New Recruit Orientation & Training Days	Days Before New Recruit Takes Customer Calls	Training Techniques Employed
A	25 days	10 days assisted	Training implements a more "learn-by-doing" training focus, in which skills and philosophies are learned in the perspective of the actual duties performed. One channel being used is "goals-based scenarios," specifically with interactive CD-ROM.
B	25 training days	15 assisted days 25 unassisted days	• Programs tied to competency models—more skills- than information-based. • Multimedia/self-directed based programs. • Heavy emphasis on effective manager coaching.
C	2 days orientation	21 days	Computer-based training
D	Inbound 24 Outbound 30 Service 30	Inbound 25 Outbound 31 Service 31	Computer-based training
E	10 days	11 assisted 18 unassisted	
F	20 days	20 days	Use of the intranet and multimedia based training are enhancing the ability to deliver training anywhere and anytime
G	1 day orientation and 14 training days	16 assisted 21 unassisted	

Some institutions even feel there is a strong correlation in call routing and the differences in learning rates by service reps. While most organizations have some type of skill-based routing in place, understanding how a call center routes calls and develops skill sets may have some influence in grasping why there are differences in turnover.

With the rapidly changing business environment of today's call centers, training has become a critical success factor for human resource mangers. Some metrics are specifically training related, for instance:

1. the cost of training a new agent,
2. the percentage of agents trained to be specialized versus universal,
3. the use of computer-based training tools, and
4. the length of initial, new-hire training periods.

GBI's banking study also found that training is moving to more electronic self-study and that most new agents are expected to start taking calls unassisted by the third or fourth week of work.

Most institutions break turnover into two components: internal movements and external movements. Internal movements occur as institutions find that the call center provides an excellent entry point into the organization. Internal movements are difficult to prevent. External movements occur for a myriad of reasons—some controllable (burnout, poor performance), others not (better salary, back to school).

In any analysis, it is important to measure both and to understand the controllable portion of turnover—what you can do as managers to reduce the damage caused by turnover in your shop.

Day-to-Day Operations

There are many metrics that can be used to measure the performance
of the human resources department. Some of the most frequently
used metrics are

1. the percent of the budget spent on human
   resources as compared to the total call center
   budget,
2. the ratio of agents to supervisors (also known
   as your span of control),
3. the annual turnover rate of front-line agents,
4. the cost of hiring a new agent,
5. call quality monitoring scores,
6. agent adherence to published schedules,
7. agent occupancy rates,
8. agent attendance rates, and
9. average call handle time.

Besides measuring various ratios, it is also important to analyze the authorities different call center agents have. We look at
authorities in four separate categories: price (i.e., fee waivers, re-
funds, etc.), operational (i.e., close accounts, open accounts), service
maintenance (e.g., real time name and address change), and problem resolution. When comparing authorities, the dollar limits for
monetary changes should be collected as well.

Management

Our experience shows a wide range in the role of first-line supervisors in handling calls (usually escalated calls) and monitoring agents.
We have found drastic differences in our work in this area. Some first-
line supervisors have between 70 and 85% of their time built into

their job for agent coaching/development. Of this, approximately 20–25% is devoted to agent monitoring, and no time is built into their schedule for handling calls. Of course, there are call centers where the first-line supervisors' primary role is handling call escalation.

What drives these differences among call centers, short of industry practice, is the technology behind call monitoring, the relative importance placed on it for coaching, and the culture within the organization for staff direction. For example, call monitoring reporting can be a paper-based system or be done online using an intranet.

Staff type	Authorization Items Limits	Amount
CSA Level I		
	Pricing rebates, fee waivers	
	Problem resolution (i.e., extend payment terms)	
	Operational (change address, close accounts, etc.) Service maintenance	
CSA Level II		
	Pricing rebates, fee waivers	
	Problem resolution (i.e., extend payment terms)	
	Operational (change address, close accounts, etc.)	
	Service maintenance	

Motivation

What the proper reward structures for motivating staff are and sharing this information in benchmarking interests many call center managers. We have found various monetary and non-monetary (e.g., voluntary time off) forms of incentives. In addition, besides individual-based performance rewards, we have found team- and center-based reward structures. Your staff members are interested in what they can make from the monetary rewards and the recognition that arises from non-monetary awards.

Our experience suggests that a reward program which is tied to quantitative data on performance and gets the staff involved in selecting best performers works best. Better-performing staff may also be used to transfer knowledge to other members who are not performing as well.

Ultimately the key to any reward program is not staff members who come to expect a certain amount in addition to salary, but that the program be viewed for what it is meant to accomplish—reward outstanding performance.

Knowledge Available to the Agents

The fastest-growing sector in call center evolution is providing agents with better and better access to mission-critical information stored elsewhere within the enterprise information technology. This is also a great area for comparison benchmarking. For instance, you might compare the following:

1. What customer information, such as customer name, address, phone number, etc., do agents have access to when a call reaches their desktop?

2. What operational knowledge, such as billing, frequently asked questions, pricing, etc., is accessible?

3. How many seconds does it take to access information?

4. Does an agent have easy access to product-specific diagnostic information with simple keyword searches?

Of course, these are just examples of fields to compare when benchmarking your call center's knowledge databases. The metrics investigated here can provide you with competitive advantages to outperform competitors, because the better you know yourself and your customer, the better you can create customer satisfaction. The figure below shows the level of capability at which others are in allowing their agents to be truly "knowledge workers."

What Customer Knowledge Do Your TSRs Have Access To?

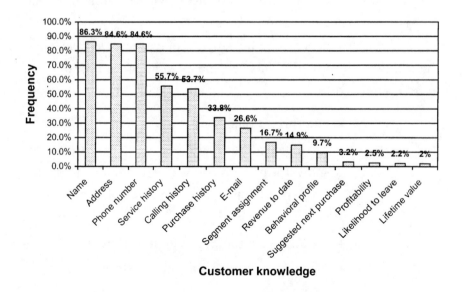

(Source: Purdue University Call Center Benchmark Study, ©1999)

As you can see from the figure on the previous page, there is a lower percentage of call centers with customer assessment/customer intelligence at the agent desktop and a higher percentage with static data, such as name and address. As we know, not all customers are the same. How customer value information is used is of interest as well. For example, when phone reps at banker First Union in Charlotte, N.C., are called, they use a special system to obtain a profile that ranks customers by balances, account activity, branch visits, and other variables. The best customers often get breaks on charges that others don't.

Benchmarking should not only include what information is presented but also how the information is displayed and the ease of access to that information. Information available via ten screens versus information available via two screens will save time and make it easier to train new recruits.

With customers calling for a myriad of reasons, we have found the following information has become more important for desktop access:

- enterprise contact history
- broadcast alert capabilities (i.e., "because of the snowstorm last night, we were not able to make the deposit cutoff time, therefore please advise customers that…")
- intranet help (product and procedures), and
- some type of profitability or customer value information.

If the information is presented to agents, call centers can use real-time marketing to treat every customer call as a possible target of a current marketing campaign. When customer identification information, such as an account or telephone number, is entered in the application, campaign processing that uses that customer's specific data can proceed immediately. In the background, campaigns you have designated for use during particular kinds of calls are targeted, matching offers or other marketing messages to the customer on the phone.

Knowledge Generated by the Call Center

What do others in your company know about your own call center? Do you generate timely reports that are of interest to your peers in other departments? This area is mostly concerned with the level of information that you as a call center have of your own operations, and what is done with this information. When comparing your level of data gathering and information production to other call centers, you can focus on the following areas:

1. Is there a formal mechanism to collect caller data?
2. Is this caller data properly warehoused?
3. Is there trained staff to process this caller data into actionable information?
4. Does caller information get disseminated to other department managers who need to know about the caller's actions in a timely fashion?

Many marketing programs can be driven from call center data, even negative ones. For example, consider the negative marketing program by Fidelity to eliminate phone calls to the call center. "In an effort to cut expenses in its huge telephone-service operation, the

No. 1 mutual-fund company has notified about 30,000 customers that they will no longer be able to reach a human being over the telephone to obtain fund balances, stock quotes, and other commonly sought information. Instead, Fidelity is telling these clients—singled out because of their frequent calling—to use its website or automated-phone system to obtain the information. Fidelity's move is part of a trend among financial-services companies using sophisticated phone technology to target less-profitable customers"

Call Center Technology

There are approximately 215 different categories of software and hardware that can be used to design and implement a truly world-class call center. Each of the 215 different categories is occupied by at least five competent suppliers, or vendors, making the choices of call center design seem both endless and difficult.

The integration of the right mix of technologies to deliver the required strategy of a call center is what differentiates the fantastic call centers from just another "also ran" call center. This is why bench-marking always includes a heavy dose of understanding what tech-nology is in place and how has it been applied to the solution of the callers' requests.

The underlying purpose of technology is to empower agents with the tools and information to service customers better. We know that selecting the right mix of technologies can have a major impact on

- reducing call lengths,
- increasing agents' knowledge of the customers' behavior and needs,

- reducing training time,
- improving service (CTI and other multimedia-distributed systems enable call centers to offer better customer service and at the same time significantly improve productivity by automating many of the call processing steps), and
- increasing customer satisfaction.

Some of the major hardware choices to benchmark are as follows:

1. automatic call distributor (ACD),
2. voice response unit (VRU),
3. interactive voice response unit (IVR),
4. computer-telephony integration (CTI),
5. predictive dialing,
6. headsets, and
7. reader boards.

Some of the major software choices to benchmark are the following:

1. automatic number identification (ANI),
2. dialed number identification service (DNIS),
3. computer-assisted telephone (CAT) survey,
4. automated e-mail software response,
5. skill-based routing, and
6. agent-monitoring software.

The Integration Challenge

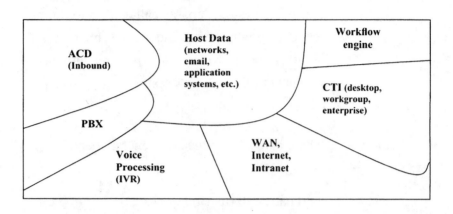

The use of all these technologies may not always be economical. The integration of a number of such systems also increases the technical complexity of the computer system. Achieving cost-effective voice/data integration through CTI requires that the customer-contact management system be integrated with VRUs, voice mail, fax, automated e-mail response, Internet, automated dialing and workforce management, and scheduling functionality.

How companies are approaching the integration challenge and the lessons they have learned are of particular interest as a qualitative exchange of information.

For example, in banking, imaging and workflow systems are being added to call centers to create callflow/workflow centers. "Loans by Phone," a standard voice response feature in banking call centers, can allow customers to apply for loans over the telephone by answering a series of questions with numeric responses on the telephone number pad. When integrated with an automated loan-processing system, once an application is filed, credit history can be obtained, profiles updated, applications scored, and decisions made before the completed application is placed in a loan officer's hands.

Technology Spending Benchmarking

Our experience in benchmarking technology spending per user suggests three precautions be taken:

1. Beware of technology cost comparisons.

    The cost accounting to support all network administration, LANs, WANs, equipment depreciation, maintenance, licenses, etc., may be spread over corporate and call center cost codes and sometimes are difficult to break out. This can lead to some very different figures (see the chart on the following page from a recent GBI bank call center study). The best way to compensate for this in any analysis is to make sure you identify those specific IT costs you would like to include and provide strict definitions of what the expense means.

2. Focus on IT headcount resources, both internal and external

    Our experience also suggests that one identify the IT support headcount (both within the call center and external, either through outsourcing parties or within the organization) that is dedicated to making sure the call center runs smoothly.

    Careful attention should be give to the management of the technology labor force, including the number, skill level, training, and organization of these key human resources. While it is difficult to correlate technology staff management practices with the efficiency of institutions, this is an area where lessons learned and best practices can be applied.

**Annual Technology Expenses per call Center Agent,
Sales and Service Agents Combined**

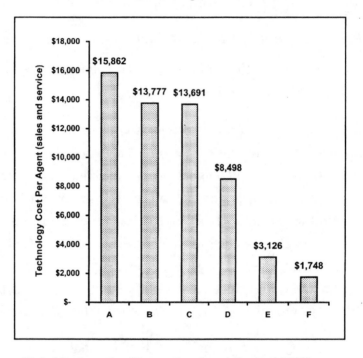

(Source: Global Business Intelligence Benchmark Study, ©1999)

3. Understand the capital budgeting process used to assess new technology spending.

Institutions have been eagerly exploring the use of newly maturing call center technologies to reach higher levels of functionality and efficiency. At the same time, trying to service customers from multiple contact points and the growing importance of call centers have put pressure on companies to further invest in new technologies to automate processes (e.g., automated e-mail response) or face ever rising headcount.

Trying to collect trend data is difficult, since much call center investment is spiked by nature (i.e., replacement software, new desktops, etc.) and occurring at a dizzying pace. We would prioritize spending areas and quantify relative investment amounts. For example, the capital budgeting and decision processes surrounding the investment in PC and Web-based service and sales can be analyzed for software and hardware platforms, third-party vendor relationships, and outsourcing decision trees.

Facilities and Design

Facilities and design refers to the environmental aspects of your workspace. As discussed before, your employees are your most valuable assets, and they need to be provided with a pleasant working environment. Good working conditions can decrease turnover rates and increase productivity, which will often increase revenues and customer loyalty.

Useful metrics to use for benchmarking this area are

1. the total number of agent seats divided by the total number of seats,
2. the average size of cubical workspace,
3. the total cubical workspace divided by the total square feet of your call center,
4. the size of the desktop screen,
5. the diagonal of the desktop computer screen, and
6. the different types of additional space that you provide for your employees (i.e., cafeteria, break room, smoking room, study room, etc.).

Researchers at Purdue University have studied the availability of spaces for the benefit of the call center employees at industrywide call centers. The chart on the following page provides you with some of these results.

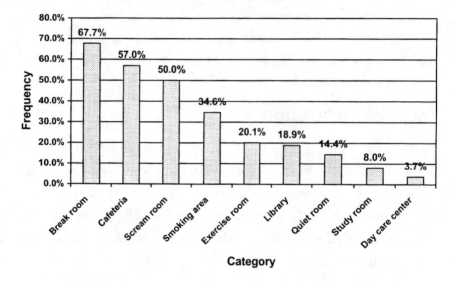

**What Types of Special Areas Are Available
for the Welfare of the Employees?**

(Source: Purdue University Call Center Benchmark Study, ©1999

Sometimes understanding the background information on the decision of where to locate call center sites is as profitable as understanding the space issues themselves. The criteria for location selection typically come down to

- proximity to markets–balance telecom and staffing costs,
- availability of part-time staff, competencies, and costs of staff,
- access to new and trainable recruits,
- technological infrastructure to support call centers,
- public transportation available for staff,
- financial incentives, and
- other corporate initiatives—"You shall be in this building."

In addition, companies are using their call centers to differentiate service among their customer base. Financial institutions generally segment their service offering by some customer segmentation. Again this is a strategic choice that is typically driven by some perception of customer value.

Example: Financial Institution Customer Segmentation

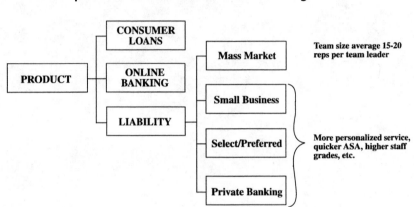

4

Benchmarking Your Call Center

Benchmarking is no easy undertaking. The experiences of several major companies demonstrate that a well-planned and executed effort can successfully open the organization to new ideas and methods, and that a poorly executed program can fail to produce any useful information (Whiting 1991).

If you believe that significant improvements can be made to a certain service, process, or practice, but you do not know what changes to make, benchmarking is the way to find out. Setting out to benchmark a service, process, or practice requires your organization to carefully scrutinize its own processes prior to jumpstarting the benchmarking effort. This chapter will provide you with the necessary steps to take in your benchmarking efforts and will show you what aspects to take into account in order to make it a success.

Ten Steps of Benchmarking

Before starting the whole benchmarking procedure, your company should create a team of about five to ten people that will conduct the benchmark study. A leader should be assigned who will take ownership of the project and who will be responsible for the communication between the team and executive management. You should realize that a single benchmark effort can take from five to twelve months and that best results will be achieved as you make it an ongoing effort.

Robert Camp, who served for years as a manager of benchmarking competency at the company that pioneered benchmarking, namely the Xerox Corporation, offers an extensive list of steps that companies can use when implementing benchmarking. We will use these steps as a basis for discussing the aspects of conducting a benchmark study of other call centers.

Step 1:   Identify and document the process, practice, or service to be benchmarked.

This first step is very important to ensure a strong focus for the benchmark research. A common mistake in benchmarking is studying too many factors and parameters simultaneously, resulting in reams of data and no actionable results. If possible, limit the benchmarking scope to something that can be finished in less than ninety days. The attention span of executives is quite short; therefore, measurable results are mandatory to ensure continued funding of the effort.

For example, start out with a targeted question that can be part of that 1% improvement. Many external consultants benchmark human resource issues given the high labor content of call center budgets and the importance of touching the customer.

- How can we automate more calls?
- How can I improve my turnover rate?
- What incentives should I be providing my service agents? Sales agents?
- How can I improve my accuracy with my staffing models?

On the other hand, if your focus is on costs, we find factors that affect call centers costs can be divided into inherent, structural, and operational costs, and data can be collected around the factors below:

Cost Type	Controllable by Operations	Driven by Market or Extraneous Circumstances
Inherent (or "What You Do")		• Scope of activities • Customer mix • Product mix
Structural	• Back office interfaces • Career-path management • Technology deployed • Call-routing methodologies • Equipment • Level of outsourcing (i.e., to handle peak call-overflow periods)	• Network locations • VRU usage
Executional	• Staff organization • Workload balancing • Scheduling • Management practices • Agent efficiency • Incentive compensation • Training	Service levels offered and achieved

Given the inherent complexities of collecting all this data, you may decide to benchmark a subset of these categories.

Sometimes your efforts are less process-oriented and more focused on understanding the strategies behind the inbound call centers. For example, you may find it is important to focus on products and services supported, the way that the call center reports in the organization, underlying business philosophies in managing the call center, the service offering to the customer base, and the scale and underlying network strategies.

**Key Business Drivers to Focus on
If Performing a Competitive Strategy Assessment**

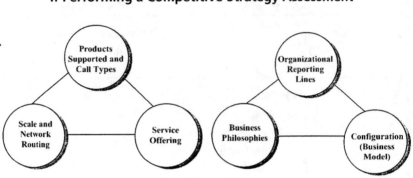

For example, in our experience with financial services call centers, we find site management ultimately reporting to the consumer bank head directly or through a retail distribution alternative delivery channel head or through a centralized operations management area. Each one of these groups will have different key criteria to emphasize and measure and, hence, improve upon.

Step 2:   Identify the company, or companies, against which you will benchmark your selected process.

This is a search process and your team should set up a list of potential companies. Thorough research of these companies is needed to narrow down the list, and then you will have a real challenge to make your final selection or selections. You may, in fact, not want to, or be able to, benchmark your direct competitors. Instead, you may want to benchmark companies that are similar. For instance, a diesel engine manufacturer may want to benchmark a chip manufacturer, as each produce and distribute an "engine" that operates inside of another company's product.

There are two critical variables under this step: 1) whether to do same- or cross-industry benchmarking and 2) whom to benchmark yourself against.

Same- or Cross-Industry Benchmarking

If your goal is to set up a systematic, ongoing comparison between yourself and competitors, benchmarking within the same industry is necessary. A call center manager interested in automating more calls to the VRU cannot compare himself or herself across industry or even within the same industry. Take the example of credit cards and general retail banking inquiries. Credit card call centers typically have truncation rates (defined as the call was answered by the VRU alone) of 30–50%. General bank call centers have truncation rates that are much higher, from 60 to 85%.

**VRU Calls as a Percent of Total Service Calls,
General Retail Banking Call Centers**

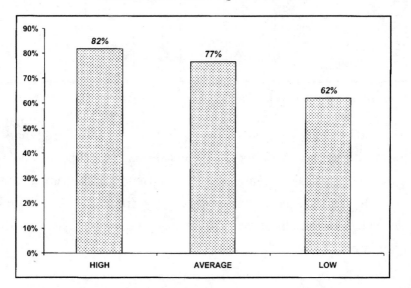

Even when doing like business, inevitably key differences will arise. For example, Global Business Intelligence's survey of top twenty banks and their retail bank call centers found all the banks supported consumer loans and retail liability products through their call centers, but only a few banks added insurance- and investment-related products. These product differences will affect how the operations design jobs, train people, and route calls. In short, there will be significant operational differences.

Products Supported/ Services Offered	Bank A	Bank B	Bank C	Bank D	Bank E	Bank F
Liability Products	•	•	•	•	•	•
Consumer Loans	•	•	•	•	•	•
Retirement Products		•	•	•	•	
Investments			•	•		
Home Equity	•	•	•		•	
ATM/debit cards		•	•	•	•	•
Insurance			•			
Support for mortgages/ credit cards (not primary call center)	•		•	•	•	

(Source: Global Business Intelligence Benchmark Study, ©1999)

It is precisely why same-industry/line-of-business benchmarking is critical. One important point to note is that these types of studies are rarely statistically significant. You just cannot get the sample size.

If your goal is to look at drastically different business processes or to think out of the box, then a cross-industry study is appropriate.

- Many business processes can be benchmarked across multiple industries.
- Some of the most dramatic learning comes from those who operate outside of your industry.
- Different industries, including non–call center industries, address the same problems in completely different ways.

In making the buy vs. conduct your own study decision under this category, our experience says there are a number of trade-offs to consider. While existing studies offer immediate results and relatively low cost compared to doing your own benchmarking project, they may not address the specific need you have. Consider conducting your own project when

- you have a very specialized area of focus;
- you have no existing data on your focus area; and/or
- it is required to support a major change project.

Benchmarking Partners

Many industries and business are becoming more concentrated. CitiGroup's credit card business is not interested in benchmarking itself against the top fifty issuers of cards in the world, but the top ten. The same is true with many other businesses. That's not to say that the number-fifty issuer is not doing innovative things, but its market share relative to CitiGroup's is insignificant.

Typically we find competitive studies must be done through third parties, or else you will not get your competitor to share confidential data.

Step 3:   Collect and store data about these companies.

Robert Camp recommends that this process should be done both internally and externally. The use of business databases that provide you with competitive intelligence, company histories, product development, and industry information is highly recommended as well.

This step has two critical components: first, what hypotheses you are starting with, which will drive your data collection; and second, how to ensure the data collection is not useless or, worse, gathering misleading information.

Countless individuals rush to collect information without first determining what hypotheses they have, which will shape what they need to collect to prove or to disprove certain beliefs.

Once you know what data you need to collect, the key becomes how to ensure it is in a consistent format. Without consistent definitions as to what is included as part of salaries and benefits (e.g., are corporate benefit overhead administration costs to be included?), what is meant by team leader, or what the formula is to determine cost per queue (is management included or just first-line supervisors?), you can arrive at some very different answers.

Finally, surveys, no matter how properly worded, will cause confusion. How we interpret words and the emphasis and meanings we place on them can be quite different. Take, for example, the question, "How many incoming calls did your call center handle?" Is that to include all calls? What about calls truncated at the VRU? What if there are multiple transactions per call? How are these calls handled?

Step 4:   Analyze the data.

Lies, damn lies, and statistics. Nowhere is that more appropriate than when trying to analyze the vast amount of data one can collect in these exercises. It is important to ensure not only that measures are defined, but also that participants use that definition and do it for the same period of time. Rarely are benchmarking studies statistically relevant for your line of business.

One example of a misunderstanding is abandoned calls. Since many times callers will do "short" abandons, (i.e., recognize they have a wrong number or don't have time to wait), collecting data on the whole process is misleading.

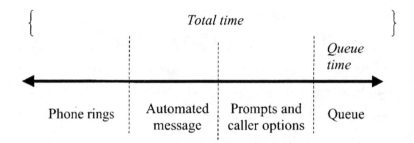

If general abandonment is requested, you may get a combination of

- short abandons,
- abandon for alternative delivery, and
- abandon out of queue.

Abandonment rate is typically defined as a call that is answered by your ACD but terminated before an agent answers it.

Further, abandonment can be a misleading measure of call center performance. The conventional wisdom is that longer queues translate into higher abandonment. But the seven factors can help explain paradoxes.

For example, when the stock market swings significantly, mutual funds and others in the financial industry get a flood of calls. Even though service level may drop, abandonment also goes down because callers have a higher degree of motivation and are willing to wait, if necessary. While this may be an obvious example, there are more subtle day-to-day shifts in caller tolerance.

By analyzing the data you will see the gaps between your company's practice and the practices of the best of the breed in your industry. You may have the opportunity to slice the data in many ways, for example, by size of call center, size of company, geography, business configuration, etc.

Step 5:   Project future performance.

Competition does not stand still, and this means that you will have to project your results beyond today's issues. This requires analysis and understanding of industry trends to see how fast you and your competition are changing. By focusing on this step properly, you will keep your results from becoming outdated too quickly.

Step 6:   Communicate the results and get acceptance within your organization.

Getting "buy in" from critical team players can be a challenge. By communicating the benchmark results, you enhance the possibility of getting acceptance from senior management and, more importantly, the employees who will be asked to make changes and improvements.

The results of benchmarking usually arrive to some quality or performance management team.

The team then communicates the results to the respective areas, which can include various sites, such as operations, technical support, and training, as well as senior management. Our experience suggests that doing something with all the information presented in a benchmarking study is the single biggest obstacle and where most companies fall short.

Example Structure in Banking

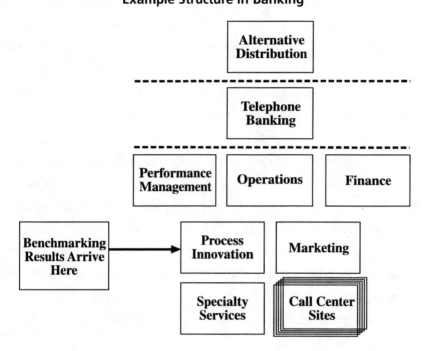

Besides the need to compare oneself with others (hence the Olympic Games), the results from these exercises can be misused or twisted in a way to meet internal objectives. For example, a call center manager may be an advocate of natural speech recognition to increase the information received by the caller. The investment for this capability on the VRU has not been supported by prior ROI analysis. Using the results of the benchmarking study, the manager may take certain facts out of context.

A problem that is even worse is when colleagues suggest the study was flawed and the results do not matter. This implies two things: 1) the participants were not active up front in determining what they wanted to learn and how they would collect the information, and 2) a passive participation on the part of the participants.

By all means, you need to take a proactive role in survey design, data collection methods, etc. This is not a passive process. If you sense that as the data is being collected it will not answer the questions you need answered, you need to understand why. Is the information too hard to collect (expense data), is some information too confidential, or is the third party not peeling the onion and getting to the right depth on certain areas?

Another area of concern is when the benchmarking team comes back and makes all kinds of claims to its management about how its operation is better than all the others. The reason for participating in these studies is not to make claims of "we're number 1," but to make continued incremental improvements in one or more areas. While it may be true that certain call centers have better productivity, costs, and/or quality numbers, the fact is that managing a call center involves managing various trade-offs.

Step 7:   Establish objectives.

After concurrence on findings and strategy, the team will have to present final recommendations on goals and how the organization must change to achieve new levels of performance.

Step 8:   Develop an action plan for each objective.

The plans should detail the tasks involved and include specific names and dates associated with each task. Everybody responsible for each process should be involved in setting up these change plans.

Step 9:   Implement and monitor the results.

This step, which is generally performed by an implementing group and its manager, is very critical. It includes collecting data on new levels of performance, using problem-solving teams to investigate issues, and adjusting the improvement process if goals are not being met.

Step 10:   Start the process over again, step by step.

Since your company, your industry, and your customers continue to change, this step is very important. How often you will have to start the process over again depends on how fast your environment is changing.

Critical Success Factors

Adhering to the steps that we explained above will not necessarily lead to a successful benchmarking effort by itself. There are certain factors every organization will have to take into account when striving to make the benchmark effort really worthwhile. Used correctly, benchmarking is a very effective tool, but if not carried out correctly, it can certainly be a very costly, time-consuming effort. Your results may show no resemblance to the true requirements of a good benchmark study, which will cause you to be unable to identify fields for improvement, and so on. Let's now consider some factors that could prevent your efforts from turning into a disaster.

First of all, the organization needs an active commitment from senior management. This means not only that upper management will know that there is a benchmark effort going on, but also that it needs to be part of the effort. As step 1 already explained, clear objectives have to be defined. Upper management plays a very important role in this part, because it is supposed to know where the company is heading. Everybody involved needs to know what your benchmark focus will be.

The introduction to this chapter already mentioned the importance of having a clear and comprehensive understanding of your own organization's strategy. Without this information, it is simply impossible to make a comparison against best practices in your industry. When benchmarking findings show that you have to make significant changes in your working processes, you need to be willing to adapt and change according to these findings. This requires a flexible organizational structure and, of course, a willingness by top management to change.

Organizations should be open to new ideas and creativity, and innovative in their applications to existing practices. Again this point shows that it is very important to have top management committed to your effort so that it will be prepared to act on changes when the time is right. Your competition is also constantly changing, and it is of urgent importance to try to stay ahead of them.

The concept of actually sharing information with your competitors may seem contradictory, but you should be willing to participate because it is a crucial part of the benchmarking effort. Wherever possible, you should be focusing on the best-in-class companies in your industry, because every step below will mean less than optimal results in the end.

To conclude this section on critical success factors, we would like to point out that adherence to the benchmarking project is vital. To achieve this, you must make the benchmark effort an initiative within your organization. This will make it easier to achieve a continuous effort and will strengthen bonds with upper management. Benchmarking will provide you with the data that you need to justify your conclusions.

The Rules

When thinking of benchmarking, people often ask themselves the following questions:

1. What is benchmarking?
2. When should you conduct a benchmark study?

3. How much preparation, time, and money does a benchmark study cost?

4. How do we choose our partners?

Although these are important questions to ask yourself, you should definitively add another, and that is, "Do I have to be aware of any legal issues?" The answer to this question is "yes." There are definitely legal matters that you should be aware of, and we will address them in this section.

First, and most important of all, benchmarking with other best-in-class organizations means that these organizations are providing you with information on how to improve. In turn, this often comes down to the fact that your organization provides reciprocal information. The transfer of information can be a very delicate issue depending on its source and content. This means that you will always have to treat the information confidentially and as if it were internal, privileged information.

The exchange of information implies that you should be willing to provide your partner(s) with the same level of information that you requested. Avoid discussions or actions that might lead to restraints of trade when studying your competitor's information on prices and costs.

Second, the use of information obtained through a benchmark partnering should be only for the purpose of improvement of operations within the partnering companies themselves. It is very important that the partner's approval be requested before using the information for external purposes. The same goes for individual information. Whenever an individual's name is requested for contact purposes, ask that person's permission to give it out before doing so. Partnering companies should initiate contracts, whenever possible, to overcome these issues. Let both (or multiple) companies agree on the written agreements.

Benchmarking is not meant to be a way to directly attack your best-in-class competitors. It is not a tool to limit competition or gain business through mutual relationships. When conducting a benchmark study, companies should set up certain ground rules up front. Both parties have to know the goal of the benchmark effort and both parties should adhere to it as well. To establish a good relationship with their partner(s), companies might refrain from asking for sensitive information. In actions between benchmarking partners the emphasis should be on trust and openness, instead of on distrust and betrayal. Organizations sometimes use an ethical external party to assemble and blind competitive data that will be used for direct competitor comparisons, and this is a good recommendation.

In short, to contribute to efficient, effective, and, moreover, ethical benchmarking, partners should keep it legal, be willing to give as they receive, respect the confidentiality issues, keep information internal, never refer to information without permission, and show up prepared at initial contacts.

We would highly recommend signing nondisclosure agreements with any third-party vendor. If the information is strategic in nature and may hurt your competitive advantage, then refrain from disclosing. This is particularly the case when discussing new initiatives, such as adding products or services supported to your call center.

5

Interpreting Call Center Benchmark Data

"One of the many unique aspects about managing a call center is that there is an abundance of easily available process measurements from which to select in establishing a management feedback and control system" (Anton 1997). The essence of this sentence has been elaborated upon before. The challenge is to see the forest from the trees now that you have decided upon what areas to benchmark and you have conducted a benchmark study of your own. This leads to even more specific information about your call center and allows you to measure gaps between the best-in-class practices and your own call center practices. This chapter will focus on the use of the collected call center benchmark data. How do you determine the gaps? How can you calculate the value of the gaps? What are possible solutions to minimize these gaps?

Same Line of Business Interpretations

Even within the same industry, you have different types of call centers. Take the banking example below, where we segment call centers into two categories, generic and monoline.

Generic Banking Call Centers

Retail call centers handle general banking calls, mostly inbound, and offer support for a wide variety of banking products. Large retail banks tend to operate many call centers with a wide geographic disbursement. The Tower Group estimates that many of the top 15 U.S. commercial banks have upwards of 20 different centers.

Monoline Banking Call Centers

These centers support single lines of business and are highly focused on providing support and sales for a specific product type, most commonly credit products (mortgages and credit cards). They handle both inbound calls (support) and outbound calls (sales). Monoline banks, many whose business is nationwide, tend to have fewer call centers but can have as many as 500 agents in some of the larger centers.

Differences between Retail Banking and Monoline Call Centers

	Call Centers	
	Retail Banking	**Monoline**
Primary contact point	IVR	Agent
IVR resolution rate	60–70%	35–45%
Role in delivery	Pivot point in multi-channel delivery strategy	Primary customer contact point
Consumer usage characteristics	Rapidly growing	Relatively mature
Current technology focus	Increasing capacity and upgrading technology	Upgrading technology

Source: The Tower Group

Let's make a basic assumption. The call center we just benchmarked supports much of the same products and services and handles many of the same type of incoming calls.

We will review three interpretations of the data depending upon whether the focus was on improving your cost structure, improving your human resource practices, or improving throughput.

Cost Structure Focus

Understanding Scale Curves

Scale curves are an analytical tool to estimate the relationship between size (scale) and unit costs. The axes are usually measured in logs to display a linear relationship and look at the cost effect of doubling volume.

Call Center Scale Economics

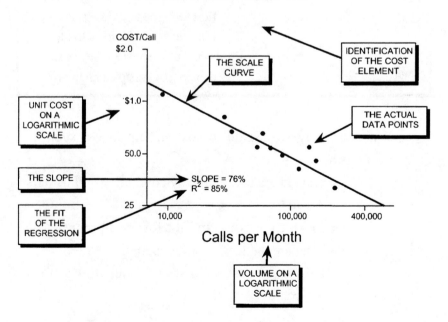

The three factors that usually affect cost are size, experience, and complexity. Each factor can be analyzed separately:

FACTOR	NAME OF TECHNIQUE	LOGIC
Size	Scale Curve	Larger size enables greater efficiency through division of labor and superior equipment. Analyzed by collecting data on number and type of transactions.
Experience (cumulative production)	Experience Curve	The more an organization produces a product or service, the more efficient it should become. Analyzed by staff tenure, management depth, and age of call center.
Complexity	Key Business Drivers	The less complex an organization (and the less time spent in internal coordination), the lower its costs. Understand key business drivers of costs (see chapter 3).

When properly used, scale curves can help answer such specific questions as

- How much can I save by combining call centers A and B?
- In which regions am I the low-cost producer?
- Who are the low-cost competitors?
- How much cost will I save if I can grow at 15% per year?

Some of the benefits of scale are listed below:

COST ITEM	BENEFITS OF SCALE
Individual piece of equipment	Spread equipment costs over larger volumes
Capital required in an entire production unit (e.g., call center)	Typically only a few pieces of equipment must be increased in size given more output
Variable costs	Better division of labor
Cost of a labor force (e.g., service agents)	As volume in a location increases, the idle time usually decreases
Anywhere where costs are fixed (i.e., supervisors, managers, etc.)	Spreading the fixed costs over a broader base

In doing scale curves in call centers, we typically look at costs by some queue and measure the variable and fixed cost elements of handling the incoming volume. As noted in chapter 3, be careful of assessing call center costs.

Other Key Cost Drivers — AHT and Service Offering

Besides volume, the single other factor having the most impact on call center costs is average handling time (AHT). Our methodology is to look at the AHT for the transactions that explain 80% of a call center operation's volume and understand what creates differences in times between the same institutions. For example, to perform an address change may take 45 seconds at call center A and 75 seconds at call center B. The difference of 30 seconds multiplied by the volume of address changes will indicate time and cost savings.

The critical step is to understand why one call center can shave 30 seconds off this transaction. In this example, it may be that a vastly higher proportion of customers enter their account number or some other form of identification (e.g., social security number) into the VRU to do a screen pop of a customer file with the agent ready and waiting, while at the other institution, the agent must ask for the information and confirm and wait for the screen.

Other measures of cost differences typically are noncontrollable. For example, given your location, your labor and rent costs are given. We find that salary, benefits, and rental rates can differ substantially across country and by industry.

Service levels are a business decision. While their impact can have an enormous effect on cost differences (a shop with an average speed of answer of 20 seconds is a higher-cost shop than one with an ASA of 60 seconds), the operation must deliver based on business needs and market conditions.

Human Resource Practices

The critical hard data areas to compare include

- compensation (salaries, benefits, incentives),
- training (recruitment and orientation, new job, on-the-job, classroom, self-study, etc.),
- turnover (external and internal),
- supervisory practices (self-manage, team-leader structure, etc.),
- idle time management (gives an idea of job burnout),

- staff tenure,
- job satisfaction (mostly done through how tasks and activities are packaged into jobs), and
- agent authorizations (what are they able to do).

Taking each one of these factors in isolation can be misleading. Knowing that your turnover is the lowest compared to your peer group may lead to incorrect conclusions if you do not realize that the low turnover is totally driven by your location (high-unemployment area versus other companies' locations). What is important in understanding HR practices is to understand how all facets of staff management come together to ensure a well-trained, cost-effective workforce and to revisit HR policies.

For example,

- How do I build jobs that reduce the monotony of constant phone work?
- What is the nature of call center jobs and how do human resource and business management strategies affect job content and quality?
- What are the proper incentive compensation schemes for agents (monetary and non-monetary), and how do they differ by agent type?

On that last example, our experience in banking call centers with incentive compensation suggests agents typically can make 10–15% more than their salary.

Example Retail Bank Service Agent Incentive Scheme

A	Reps have an opportunity to make $2,500–$2,800 per year. Based upon: 1) the representative's scores from internal call monitoring, and 2) schedule adherence.
B	Incentives based on call quality (9 calls monitored per quarter) and productivity. Paid quarterly.
C	A peer-nomination program is used to recognize exceptional service. An incentive program where the goal for service representatives is up to 10–12% of their base pay for the year, based entirely on the quality of the interaction as measured by call monitoring.
D	Up to $200/agent per month and quarterly payments of $150 for top agents.
E	Monthly recognition $250/$500 quarterly; up to $2,000 per year.

Source: Global Business Intelligence Financial Services Benchmarking Study, 1999

Productivity

While some call centers place a huge emphasis on call agent productivity, the reality is that there are some particular concerns with a "productivity only" focus.

First, you may have a productive labor force as measured by calls per agent per hour but one that is high-cost given your location, turnover, etc.

Second, customer service and quality may suffer. Customers may sense a focus on speed and not on their problems.

Third, your staff may suffer, and the results may show up in higher turnover, unexcused absences, etc.

In benchmarking productivity measures, the first question to address is to understand what key measures others focus on when it comes to productivity and the priority given to those measures. There could be a wide range. For example, compare three institutions' productivity measures below (actual measures used) and note differences.

A	1. VRU resolution rate: specific goals for individual product lines (performance is reported daily to senior management) 2. Schedule adherence and AHT monitored as KPI
B	1. Service levels: percent of calls answered in 20% (by customer segment) 2. Consistency in making targeted service level 3. Percent of days in month making targeted service level 4. Average handle time trends (by customer segment) 5. Productivity/shrinkage: availability of agents in various states 6. Schedule adherence
C	1. Calls per half hour 2. Service quality (unit managers' goals incorporate both measurements)

Note that institution A is more focused on VRU resolution and schedule adherence while institution C focuses on productivity (calls per half hour) and service quality measured. Institution B is much more focused on service by customer segment.

Call Center Performance Metrics
What Are Your Inbound Call Center Service Level Statistics?

Metric Description	Median	*Average*	Standard Deviation	Your Value
Speed of answer (seconds)	25.0	36.0	40.5	
Talk time (minutes)	3.3	*4.3*	3.2	6.2
After call work time (minutes)	1.2	*3.2*	8.8	2.7
Calls abandoned	4.3%	5.4%	5.1%	
Time in queue (seconds)	30.0	49.7	60.8	
Calls closed on first contact	83.0%	78.3%	20.3%	
Percent calls blocked	4.84%	7.97%	10.23%	
TSR occupancy	80.0%	76.0%	16.7%	
Time before abandoning (seconds)	50.0	69.5	75.7	
Adherence to schedule	92.0%	90.2%	9.6%	
Attendance	92.0%	86.2%	19.7%	
Inbound calls per 8-hour shift per TSR	65.0	74.6	64.8	

(Source: Purdue Call Center Benchmark Study, ©1999)

The table on the previous page is a very good example of a way to present the benchmark findings. The table was taken from the 1999 Purdue Call Center Benchmark Report and shows the average world-class practices of about 15 different U.S. industries and their call centers. A table like this provides you with the opportunity to compare your call center data against industry standards. This allows you to identify gaps quickly and can provide you with far more information than you might expect at first. Performance gaps have values, which you can easily calculate. An example of this will be shown later in this chapter. Gaps are costly and that is why call centers should try to close them. After the cost of a gap is determined, management will have to take further operational steps to close it. The following section will show an example of how to calculate a gap and will provide you with possible solutions to overcome the gap.

Calculating the Value of a Gap

To calculate the value of a gap you will first have to run a self-assessment to get the performance gap. Basically this comes down on the following steps:

1. Select a metric. For the purpose of this example we will take average handle time (AHT). AHT is an internal metric that can be defined as the sum of talk time and after-call work time. The automatic call distributor (ACD) can provide you with the AHT, and it is strongly suggested you run this information daily and investigate it weekly and monthly. For convenience, these figures are printed in italics in the table above.

2. Now that the metric has been selected, the next

step is to calculate your value. The value for AHT, for instance, could be easily derived from the reports that come from the ACD.

3. Third, the industry standard has to be found. This is where benchmarking comes in. Your benchmark report should be able to provide you with this information.

4. To get to the performance gap, the only thing left to do is to subtract the two numbers. The basis for your gap calculation has now been set.

Now you can continue calculating the value of the gap. To provide you with an example, the following assumptions have been made:

- We use the metric AHT.
- The gap from the table above equals 2.5 minutes.

  Your AHT value => 6.2 minutes + 2.7 minutes = 8.9 minutes *(see table)*.

  The industry average AHT value => 4.4 minutes + 2.0 minutes = 6.4 minutes *(see table)*.

  Performance gap = 8.9 – 6.4 = 2.5.
- The call center has 100 agents.
- We assume that the agents handle 50 calls per shift.
- The agents earn $10 per hour.
- The call center has one shift per day and 260 shifts per year.
- The handle costs are $0.16 per minute.

The gap value can be calculated as follows. Based upon the

above-stated assumptions, the call center would be making 5,000 calls (100 agents times 50 calls). Therefore, 12,500 minutes would be lost because of the gap (5,000 × 2.5). The center would incur extra costs of $2,083 per shift (12,500 × $0.16), and this would add up to a total gap value of $541,667 per year ($2,083 × 260 shifts).

As the example above shows, these gaps can add up to a tremendous waste of money. Every division of the call center should be aware of these gaps, and action should be taken to overcome these losses. Improvement in these areas will strengthen the call center's competitive advantage and increase performance to a best-practices level. The following section will discuss some of the possible solutions to overcome the AHT gap discussed the example above.

Suggested Management Actions

Improving performance in a certain area in the call center cannot be delegated to one person in particular. It involves many people in the area, and in the case of decreasing your AHT, we can distinguish among the call center manager, the call center supervisors, the HR manager, the information technology manager, and the telecommunications manager for instance. From the book *Call Center Management: By the Numbers,* we learn that several management actions are needed to improve the AHT of your call center.

Call Center Manager

The call center manager should track a trend line. Preferably this trend should be flat to slightly decreasing, and this line should be visible center-wide. It is important that front-line supervisors report every variance outside the target range to the call center manager. Training to increase technical product details or telephone handling skills can be required.

Call Center Supervisors

For the supervisors a large AHT indicates that too few (or too many) agents were scheduled. The scripting for the agents may be inaccurate or inadequate and their adherence to scheduled time can be low. Calls should be monitored, and it is the job of the supervisors to investigate variances and explain them to the call center agents.

HR Manager

HR managers should be aware of current trends and recruiting standards. In the training field, the focus on tactfully ending calls when the transaction is complete, more training about the products and services, and increasing the access of agents to information in databases are all facets to take into account. This requires working closely with the supervisors to identify other remedial training needs. Employees can listen to each other's calls to discover best practices to remain within the targeted range.

Information Technology Manager

The IT manager should ensure that technology keeps up with the standard of delivering timely and accurate information. It is hard to keep up with technology changes, but ensuring that the correct data is provided at any time should be a priority.

Telecommunications Manager

The switch technology should not create transfer issues. Good communication is vital to overcome and prevent performance gaps. It is very important that the different departments communicate their operations through every channel of the organization. If, for instance, production has launched a new product, the call center may not readily know how to answer questions related to this new product, which in its turn will increase AHT.

6

Conclusions

Benchmarking, the structured, analytical process of continuously identifying, comparing, deploying, and reviewing best practices worldwide, has become an indispensable tool for many call centers to maintain or create their competitive advantage. It is a powerful key tool for improvement and productivity. "Leading businesses want to retain their status as 'best-in-class' and other businesses want to achieve that status" (McNair and Leibfried 1992). It helps you to expose areas where improvement is needed, pinpoints areas of cost reduction, assesses performance objectively, and shows whether your improvement programs have been successful.

Benchmarking is a tool that is applicable to every part of the organization. Applicable areas for benchmarking your call center are costs; performance measurements; caller satisfaction measurement; call center strategy; HR management, processes and knowledge; technology; and facilities and design.

The benchmarking process can be outsourced to proven consultants, but you can also perform a benchmark study of your own. The steps to conduct a benchmark of your call center against others have been discussed. There are rules to keep in mind. You should strive to conduct efficient, effective, and, moreover, ethical benchmarking. Partners are advised to keep it legal, be willing to give everything they have, and, most important of all, respect confidentiality.

Once the benchmark data has been successfully collected, the results have to be interpreted. Good communication is vital to understand and to prevent performance gaps. By understanding the gaps, the tactical and strategic reasons for the gap can be segmented and an action plan can be set.

It is important to realize that benchmarking is not in itself a solution to a process-improvement problem. It is not just copying or catch-up, and it definitively is not quick and easy. Trying to implement best-in-class processes from other call centers requires adopting their paradigm as well (D. Appleton 1994). Benchmarking can be seen as the process of being humble enough to admit that somebody else is better at something, and being wise enough to learn how to be as good as, or even better than, them. Global competition will keep increasing, technology will change faster than ever, and as a result the need for a competitive advantage will be bigger than ever. Benchmarking (when conducted properly) can help your call center gain that advantage through improved performance and productivity.

Appendix

Call Center Benchmark Studies

- Purdue University Benchmark Research Website
  http://www.e-Interactions.com

- Purdue University Call Center Benchmark Report
  (January 1999)
  - Center for Customer Driven Quality
  - 1262 Matthews Hall, Suite 118
  - West Lafayette, IN 47906-1262
  - Tel: 1-765-494-9933
  - Fax: 1-765-494-0287

- Federal Consortium Benchmark Study Report
  (February 1995)
  - For sale by the U.S. Government Printing Office
  - Superintendent of Documents
  - Mail Stop SSOP
  - Washington, D.C. 20402-9328
  - ISBN 0-16-045578-2

- Global Business Intelligence
  Financial Services Consortium Studies
  Ste 300, 1497 Marine Dr.
  West Vancouver, B.C. V7T 1B8
  Canada
  Tel: 1-604-924-0851
  http://www.globalbanking.com

- TARP Benchmarking Study
  Attributes of World-Class Call Centers (June 1994)
  For sale by TARP
  1600 Wilson Blvd., Suite 1400
  Arlington, VA 22209
  Tel: 1-703-524-1456

- 1996 Customer Service Compensation Study
  For sale by ICSA
  401 N. Michigan Ave.
  Chicago, IL 60611-4267
  Tel: 1-800-360-4272

- 1996 SOCAP Salary & Job Description Study
  For sale by SOCAP
  801 N. Fairfax St., Suite 404
  Alexandria, VA 22314
  Tel: 1-703-519-3700

- Call Center Managers Forum
  Benchmarking reviews, web conferences on call
  center issues, case studies, and useful articles
  http://www.callcentres.com.au

References

Anderson, B., and P. G. Petterson. *The Benchmarking Handbook.* London: Chapman & Hall, 1996.

Anton, J. *Call Center Management: By the Numbers.* West Lafayette, Ind.: Purdue University Press, 1997.

Appleton, D. S. "Benchmarking . . . A Cure for 'Functional Fixedness.'" *The Business Engineer,* September 1994.

Boxwell, R. J., Jr. *Benchmarking for Competitive Advantage.* New York: McGraw-Hill, 1994.

Camp, R. C. *Benchmarking: The Search for Industry Best Practices That Lead to Superior Performance.* Milwaukee, Wis.: ASQC Quality Press, 1989.

———. *Business Process Benchmarking: Finding and Implementing Best Practices.* Milwaukee, Wis.: ASQC Quality Press, 1995.

Czarnecki, M. T. *Managing by Measuring: How to Improve Your Organization's Performance through Effective Benchmarking.* New York: Amacom, 1999.

Davis, R. I., and A. D. Roxy. *How to Prepare for and Conduct a Benchmark Project.* Department of Defense, The Electronic College of Process Innovation, 1994.

Department of Defense. *The Benchmarking Code of Conduct.* The Electronic College of Process Innovation.

Finnigan, J. P. *The Manager's Guide to Benchmarking*. San Francisco, Calif.: Jossey-Basser Publishers, 1996.

McNair, C. J., and K. Leibfried. *Benchmarking: A Tool for Continuous Improvement*. New York: HarperBusiness, 1992.

Schwartz, K. D. "Benchmarking for Dollars." *Datamation* 44 (February 1998): 50–52.

Spendolini, M. J. *The Benchmarking Book*. New York: Amacom, 1992.

Vaziri, H. K. "Using Competitive Benchmarking to Set Goals." *Quality Progress* 25 (October 1992): 81–85.

Watson, G. H. *Strategic Benchmarking: How to Rate Your Company's Performance against the World's Best*. New York: John Wiley and Sons, 1993.

Whiting, R. "Benchmarking: Lessons from the Best-in-Class." *Electronic Business* 17 (October 7, 1991): 128.

Wiesendanger, B. "Benchmarking for Beginners." *Sales and Marketing Management* 144 (November 1992): 59–64.

Index

About the Authors

Jon Anton is with the Department of Consumer and Family Sciences at Purdue University and a researcher in the Purdue Center for Customer-Driven Quality. He specializes in enhancing customer service strategy through inbound call centers and teleweb centers using the latest in telecommunications (voice), and computer (digital) technology, as well as the Internet, for external customer access along with the Intranet and middleware for organizing and delivering company information now stored in limited access databases and legacy systems.

For the past five years, Anton has been the principal investigator of the annual Purdue University Call Center Benchmark Research Report. This data is now collected at http://www.e-Interactions.com and then placed into a data warehouse with over one million data points on call center and teleweb center performance. Based on the analysis of this data, Jon authors "The Purdue Page" in *CallCenter Magazine* each month.

. Anton has assisted over 400 companies in improving their customer service strategy/delivery by the design and implementation of inbound and outbound call centers, as well as in the decision-making process of using teleservice providers for maximizing service levels while minimizing costs per call. In August of 1996, *Call-*

Center Magazine honored Dr. Anton by selecting him as an Original Pioneer of the emerging call center industry.

Dr. Anton has guided corporate executives in strategically repositioning their call center as robust customer access centers through a combination of re-engineering, consolidation, out-sourcing, and Web enablement. The resulting single point of contact for the customer allows business to be conducted anywhere, anytime, and in any form. By better understanding the customer lifetime value, Jon has developed techniques for calculating the ROI for customer service initiatives.

Dr. Anton has published 48 papers on customer service and call center methods in industry journals. In 1997, one of his papers on self-service was awarded the best article of the year by the magazine *Customer Relationship Management*. Dr. Anton has published five professional books: *Inbound Customer Call Center Design* (Dame Publishers, 1994), *Customer Relationship Management* (Prentice-Hall, 1996), *Computer-Assisted Learning* (Hafner Publishing, 1985), *Call Center Management: By the Numbers* (Purdue University Press, 1997), and *The Voice of the Customer* (Alexander Research & Communications, 1997). Dr. Anton is the senior editor for a series of professional books entitled "Customer Access Management" published by the Purdue University Press.

Dr. Anton's formal education was in technology, including a doctorate of science and a master of science from Harvard University, a master of science from the University of Connecticut, and a bachelor of science from the University of Notre Dame. He also completed a three-summer intensive executive education program in business at the Graduate School of Business of Stanford University.

David Gustin is the director for Global Business Intelligence's research programs and an internationally recognized strategy and operations consultant with 16 years' experience in banking and management consulting to the financial services industry. Mr. Gustin has extensive experience worldwide. He has worked with over 20 financial institutions on various strategic and operational assignments in North America, Asia, Europe, and Australia/New Zealand. His knowledge of banking, consulting, and technology provides a unique blend to his assignments.

Mr. Gustin's wide range of financial services experience has included assistance from strategy to implementation for a wide number of businesses and delivery channels—including payment systems, credit cards, consumer lending, trade services, cash management, commercial loan operations, branch banking, and call centers.

In addition to being the editor of the Workflow and Imaging Solution Explore (WISE) Advisory Program, David writes several articles a year for publications such as *Knowledge Management, American Banker,* and *Banking Strategies.* He is also a speaker at numerous conferences, including the Association of Imaging and Information Management Professionals, the Bankers Association of Foreign Trade, the Bankers Association Institute, Incoming Call Center Management, and various technology vendors' client conferences.

He is a former VP of Security Pacific National Bank, VP of Mellon Bank, and management consultant for Booz-Allen & Hamilton. Mr. Gustin's formal education includes an information systems degree from Carnegie-Mellon University, an MBA from Purdue University, and a CFA designation.

Stijn Spit, or "Stan," is a visiting scholar at Purdue University in the Center for Customer-Driven Quality. Mr. Spit came to Purdue as part of an organized scholarship program whereby students come from abroad to study with Jon Anton for up to six months. Upon the completion of his degree from the University of Maastricht, Stan will pursue a career in call center and teleweb-based customer service management and consulting.